Israel's Missed Opportunities ... and lost privileges

Charles Ozanne

ISBN: 978-1-78364-475-9

www.obt.org.uk

****

THE OPEN BIBLE TRUST
Fordland Mount, Upper Basildon,
Reading, RG8 8LU, UK.

Israel's Missed Opportunities
... and lost privileges

Contents

Page

Introduction

Introduction

It is with no sense of complacency or superiority that I turn to the subject of Israel's missed opportunities. I too have missed heaven-sent opportunities, failures which rankle me to the present day. Fortunately my failures are not written on tablets of stone for all to read (!), unlike Israel's which are all recorded in Scripture for our admonition and learning. The most disastrous of Israel's missed opportunities was their failure to recognise their Messiah. They rejected Him when He graced them with His presence for three and a half years, and they rejected Him in the years following when the truth of His messiahship was persuasively proclaimed to them by His faithful disciples. The abiding consequences of their unbelief are still evident today.

This was certainly the most serious of Israel's missed opportunities. There were however many others stretching back to the beginning of their national history. Israel's failure in the New

Testament is seen in perspective when placed alongside their failures in the Old Testament. I propose therefore to demonstrate how Israel's promised time of rest was offered them time and again in the course of their long history, only to be forfeited on each occasion. God however has not given up on His erstwhile people. Once more in the future they will be given a final opportunity to receive the Lord Jesus as their Messiah, and this time they will unreservedly accept Him, and with what marvellous results!

> "For if their rejection is the reconciliation of the world, what will their acceptance be but life from the dead?" (Romans 11:15).

If Joshua had given them rest ...

If Joshua had given them rest ...

Hebrews 3 and 4 speak of a time of rest which remains for the people of God (Hebrews 3:11,18; 4:1,3,5,6,8,9,10,11). It is called a Sabbath-rest or Sabbath-keeping because it is identified with God's rest, the rest which He assumed on the seventh day of creation and has continued ever since. This rest He will share with His people in the future, at the second coming of Christ. Christians of Jewish stock, such as those to whom Hebrews was written, will experience God's rest for themselves in the New Jerusalem, while those still in their earthly bodies will savour God's rest in the transformed land and city of prophetic vision and promise (Hebrews 11:10,16; 12:22).

This Sabbath-rest was on offer to God's people in the first century AD when Hebrews was written. We find there repeated warnings to those addressed not to harden their hearts, to avoid at all costs

> "a sinful, unbelieving heart that turns away from the living God" (Hebrews 3:12).

It is implied that the promised time of rest could easily be forfeited if the message was not wholeheartedly received (Hebrews 4:1-2). And this of course is precisely what happened. Those who believed were all too prone to waver and stumble while the majority of their compatriots remained adamant in unbelief. The time of rest was not experienced at that time, and so …

> "there remains, then, a Sabbath-rest for the people of God" (Hebrews 4:9).

But this was not the first occasion on which this offer was made, for we read …

> "if Joshua had given them rest, God would not have spoken later about another day." (Hebrews 4:8)

They could therefore have entered into God's rest at the time of the Conquest under Joshua. If all the Israelites had shown the same faith and courage as Joshua and Caleb, it would no doubt have materialized at that time. God however was angry with that generation. He said,

> "Their hearts are always going astray, and they have not known my ways. So I declared on oath in my anger 'They shall never enter my rest.'" (Hebrews 3:10-11, *NIV*; quoting Psalm 95:10-11)

When Jacob spoke of "the last days" (Genesis 49:1) he was not thinking of a time in the far distant future[1]. His vision extended no further than the future conquest of Canaan, when his descendants would take possession of the land promised to his father and grandfather. This happened only 240 years later, and it might have

---

[1] For a fuller treatment of the expression 'last days' see Michael Penny's *The Last Days! When?* It does not always refer to the days leading up to Christ's return but can, in some

happened only 200 years later if they had entered the land from Kadesh-Barnea as was God's original intention (Numbers 13-14).

places, refer simply to some period of time in the future.

In
David

In David

God again set a certain day, calling it "Today", when a long time later He spoke through David,

> "Today, if you will hear his voice, do not harden your hearts" (Hebrews 4:7).

These words are from Psalm 95 which is referred to more than once in the previous chapter.

The words "in David" seem to confirm that this psalm was written by David. It is in fact ascribed to David in the Septuagint from which the writer is quoting, though in the Hebrew text it is anonymous.

So the promised time of rest was again on offer and could have been appropriated when the monarchy was established under the banner of David and Solomon. Again, if all the people (or even some of them) had been as faithful and courageous as David, it might well have been established at that time. This however was not the case and once more the opportunity was forfeited.

Immanuel

Immanuel

There is some doubt when the next offer of entering God's rest was made. It could have been in the first year of King Ahaz when Isaiah was inspired to give his enigmatic prophecy to the doubting king:

> "The virgin will be with child and will give birth to a son, and will call him Immanuel. He will eat curds and honey when he knows enough to reject the wrong and choose the right" (Isaiah 7:14-15).

If this refers to the imminent birth of Christ, as many commentators think, an offer was being made in that critical situation of deliverance and ultimate Messianic rest through faith in God's promise.

Ahaz however had already made up his mind to appeal to the king of Assyria for deliverance from his enemies Rezin of Aram and Pekah king of Israel, and so the promise of salvation by

Immanuel, the virgin's Son, was rejected by King Ahaz and his advisers. Again the offer of entering into God's rest was forfeited at that time.[2]

---

[2] For more on this see *The Book of Immanuel (Isaiah 7-12)* by Charles Ozanne, published by The Open Bible Trust

After the Exile: Isaiah 40-66

After the Exile: Isaiah 40-66

This much is certain. Israel was given another opportunity during their period of exile in Babylon. Isaiah, Jeremiah and Ezekiel all spoke as if the promised time of rest would come in at the end of the Exile.

The later chapters of Isaiah are much misunderstood. Conservative scholars are agreed that they were written by the eighth century prophet, Isaiah son of Amos. They think he was thrown forward in spirit to several different points in the future. At one moment he is speaking to the exiles in Babylon, at another to the returned community in Palestine after the exile is over. In other places he is thrown forward to the end of the age, long after the Suffering Servant of the Lord had died for the sins of the people, and is addressing the nation just before their final deliverance and restoration. This however is not at all the way Isaiah saw it. For him the final and complete restoration of Israel should have occurred at the end of the Babylonian exile under the auspices of the Persian king, Cyrus, who is mentioned by name.

This was Israel's next great opportunity. If the destruction of Jerusalem and ensuing exile had had the desired effect in terms of repentance and humble confession, their full restoration could have materialized without further delay when the exile came to an end.

In Isaiah 39 Hezekiah was forewarned of the impending exile to Babylon.

> "Hear the word of the Lord Almighty: The time will surely come when everything in your palace, and all that your fathers have stored up until this day, will be carried off to Babylon. Nothing will be left, says the Lord" (Isaiah 39:5-7).

In the next chapter Isaiah is thrown forward in spirit to the end of this period of exile and addresses the people (both at home and in

Babylon) with words of comfort and hope. And this, if I am not greatly mistaken, remains his spiritual stance for the rest of the book.

The stage is set in the first two verses.

> "Comfort, comfort my people, says your God. Speak tenderly to Jerusalem, and proclaim to her that her hard service has been completed, that her sin has been paid for, that she has received from the Lord's hand double for all her sins" (Isaiah 40:1-2).

Their sin has been paid for, as in Leviticus 26:41,43. The meaning is,

> "the punishment of their iniquity has been accepted as satisfactory."

In the words of Alec Motyer,

> "the period of duress can be identified with the Babylonian captivity (Isaiah 43:14) and the satisfactory payment with the sacrifice

of the Servant of the Lord (Isaiah 52:13 ff.)."

This message of comfort is sent to Jerusalem. Jerusalem has received double for her sins, but she is not uninhabited. While Babylon is mentioned four times (Isaiah 43:14; 47:1; 48:14,20), it is Jerusalem which is primarily addressed in all these chapters. Her situation is certainly dire: forsaken and forgotten (Isaiah 49:14), afflicted, storm-tossed and uncomforted (Isaiah 54:11), cruelly treated and oppressed by her tormentors (Isaiah 51:23), caught and faint like an antelope in a net (Isaiah 51:20), and living in constant terror because of the wrath of the oppressor (Isaiah 51:13).

This is the Jerusalem of prophetic foresight, not the Jerusalem of past history; Jerusalem as it might have been, not as in fact it was. This is a point of tremendous importance since, according to Isaiah's view of the future, the redemptive suffering of the Servant had already taken place. It is this which gives meaning to Isaiah's repeated assurances that Israel's sin has been paid for, that her redemption has been accomplished (Isaiah 40:2; 44:22-23; 48:20; 52:9). The title *Goel*, Redeemer, is applied thirteen times to the Lord in these chapters. It is the fact that redemption has already been accomplished which provides the moral basis for Israel's restoration. Without it the restoration would not be possible.

This might suggest that Isaiah's prophetic stance is subsequent to the crucifixion of Christ, later than AD 32 or 33. But this is to misunderstand Isaiah's programme for the future. The fact that Cyrus is mentioned by name ties it down to the sixth century BC. Cyrus' rise to power is represented as already in the past (Isaiah 41:2,25; 45:1).

Isaiah's stance therefore is subsequent to Cyrus' meteoric rise to power, but before his conquest of Babylon (Isaiah 48:14-15) and before his command to rebuild Jerusalem and the Temple (Isaiah 44:28; 45:13). It follows therefore that the sacrificial death of the Servant, in Isaiah's prophetic vision, must have already taken place before the end of the Babylonian exile.

It has been noticed by a number of writers that Isaiah's standpoint, in the crucial passage 52:13 to 53:12, is midway between the suffering of the Servant and His future exaltation.

This may be inferred from the significant shift in tenses which has often been remarked on. Here the introduction (Isaiah 52:13-15) and the conclusion (Isaiah 53:10b-12), where the future vindication and triumph of the Servant are described, are in the future (imperfect) tense, whereas the intervening verses, where His sufferings are portrayed, are in the past (or perfect) tense. This change of tense from the future to the past and back again cannot be accidental or unimportant. The explanation must be that of J. Skinner in *The Cambridge Bible for Schools & Colleges*:

> "The standpoint assumed is therefore intermediate between the death of the Servant and his exaltation; and the great revulsion of feeling in the mind of the

speakers is not the result of the revelation of his glory, but is brought about by reflexion on his unparalleled sufferings, and his patient demeanour under them, preparing the people to believe the predictions which had hitherto seemed incredible."

The imperfect tense in Isaiah 53:10 ("though you (the Lord) make his life a guilt-offering") is only grammatical. As Alec Motyer says, it

"covers situations where the event is not in doubt but the timing is indefinite."

From Isaiah's standpoint the guilt-offering had already taken place, while the rest of the sentence belongs to the future:

"He will see his offspring and prolong his days, and the will of the Lord will prosper in his hand."

In the later chapters of Isaiah (56-66) the Suffering Servant of the past has become the

Anointed Conqueror of the future (see 59:15 - 63:6), but the time-frame has not changed. The final restoration of Israel at the close of the exilic period is still in the forefront of Isaiah's expectations.

Cyrus

Cyrus

Cyrus' career of conquest is represented as having already begun (Isaiah 41:2-4). It is the Lord who has stirred him up from the north and from the east (41:2,25; 46:11), granting him victory at every step and subduing kings before him (41:2). By means of Cyrus the Lord will destroy the imperial city of Babylon, breaking in pieces its magnificent gates of bronze and cutting asunder the bars of iron (43:14; 45:2; 48:14). In so doing he will release the Jewish captives (45:13), and command the rebuilding of Jerusalem and its temple (44:28; 45:13). Though initially ignorant of the Lord (45:4), he would come to know Him through the mighty acts which the Lord will do on his behalf (45:3), and he will call on His name (41:25). He is called the Lord's shepherd (44:28), His anointed whose right hand He grasps (45:1), the man of the Lord's counsel (46:11), he whom the Lord loved (48:14).

In the words of A.B. Davidson,

"the Assyrian and the Babylonian were mere instruments in Jehovah's hand, which He flung away, or broke in pieces like a rod, when His purpose with them was served. Cyrus is no mere instrument, he is the Lord's 'anointed' or Messiah, whose right hand He holds, whom he loveth, whom He goes before and prospers, whom He called by name when he did not know Him, and who shall even call upon His name." (*Old Testament Prophecy*, 1904, p.398.)

There is no suggestion of course that Cyrus could be *the* Messiah. The word *meshiah* , anointed, is used chiefly of Israel's kings and princes. Only in Daniel 9:25,26 is it used explicitly of the coming Messiah. Cyrus however is the only foreign prince to be called *meshiah*, anointed. Moses and David are the only other persons given the title of Shepherd (Isaiah 63:11; Ezekiel 34:23; 37:24). The expression "the Lord loved him" (*Yahweh ahevo*) is used elsewhere only of the Lord's love for the infant Solomon (2 Samuel 12:24). The Cyrus of prophetic anticipation far excels the

Cyrus of historical reality.

The Cyrus of history is known to us from the books of Ezra and Daniel and from his own inscriptions. His victorious entry into Babylon on 16 Tishri (12 October), 539 BC is mentioned in both the Cyrus Cylinder and the Nabonidus Chronicle. In both it is emphasized that he entered Babylon unopposed without a battle, and that Babylon was spared a calamity. This also is how it is depicted in Daniel 5. As for the predictions that Cyrus would rebuild both city and temple, Motyer says,

> "This is exactly what happened (Ezra 1:1-5; 6:1-5)."

But it was not really so. Cyrus' decree to rebuild the Temple was never implemented in his lifetime. It was not till the second year of Darius, 18 years later, that a start was made on the Temple, and not till the twentieth year of Artaxerxes, 93 years later, that the rebuilding of the city was authorized. Cyrus' decree never mentioned the city at all, contrary to Isaiah's prediction.

Far be it from me to cast doubt on the veracity of God's word, but it needs to be recognized that Isaiah's vision of Israel's redemption and restoration by the end of the Babylonian exile was never fulfilled. It undoubtedly *could* have happened exactly as predicted if Israel's punishment had induced the desired response of repentance and contrition in the afflicted nation.

The Lord explains in Hosea what should have happened after Ephraim and Judah had been torn to pieces and carried off into exile:

> "Then I will go back to my place until they admit their guilt. And they will seek my face; in their misery they will earnestly seek me" (Hosea 5:15).

There follows the very words the Lord would have liked to hear from the lips of His repentant people,

> "Come, let us return to the Lord. He has

torn us to pieces but he will heal us; he has injured us but he will bind up our wounds … Let us acknowledge the Lord; let us press on to acknowledge him."

There will of course come a time when Israel will respond in precisely the manner recorded here (Zechariah 12:10-14). But that was not their response to the destruction of Jerusalem in 586 BC and their subsequent hardship in Babylon. The exiles (for the most part) were perfectly happy to settle down in their new environment and to carry on life and business as before.

When permission was granted for their return to Palestine, comparatively few took advantage of the offer. The majority were content to remain in Babylonia.

Daniel was one who besought the Lord in profound misery and repentance on behalf of his people (Daniel 9), but there were few who followed his worthy example. In the circumstances there could be no final restoration of Israel in 538-36 BC, no realization of their promised Sabbath-rest. This was another opportunity which they allowed to pass unheeded and unrepented.

Most of Isaiah's forecast of future events will still take place at the end of the age when Israel is restored. But we should not expect another Cyrus to appear, one who matches up to the Cyrus of Isaianic anticipation. The suffering of the Lord's Servant was fulfilled, as we know, in the crucifixion of Christ. Isaiah however expected it to happen in course of the Babylonian exile, not in Babylon as some have supposed, but among the oppressed community left behind in Judah.

At an earlier date he had expected Immanuel to be born and live in a land overrun and occupied by the Assyrian invader (Isaiah 7-8). In the fulness of time He was born and lived in similar circumstances, in a land occupied and ruled by the Roman invader. His coming was announced at various times, but the true timing was not revealed to Isaiah or to any other pre-exilic prophet.

Jeremiah

Jeremiah

Jeremiah's prophetic programme of future events is declared in the clearest possible terms. This programme, in outline at least, was revealed to Jeremiah in 605 BC which was both the fourth year of King Jehoiakim of Judah and the first year of King Nebuchadnezzar of Babylon (25:1). It is stated as follows in Jeremiah 25:8-14:-

> Therefore the Lord Almighty says this: 'Because you have not listened to my words, I will summon all the peoples of the north and my servant Nebuchadnezzar king of Babylon,' declares the Lord, 'and I will bring them against this land and its inhabitants and against all the surrounding nations. I will completely destroy them and make them an object of horror and scorn, and an everlasting ruin. I will banish from them the sounds of joy and gladness, the voices of bride and bridegroom, the sound of millstones and the light of the lamp. This whole country will become a desolate

wasteland, and these nations will serve the king of Babylon for seventy years. But when the seventy years are fulfilled, I will punish the king of Babylon and his nation, the land of the Babylonians, for their guilt,' declares the Lord, 'and will make it desolate for ever ... They themselves will be enslaved by many nations and great kings; I will repay them according to their deeds and the work of their hands.'

The restoration of Israel at the end of the seventy years is stated in Jeremiah 29:10-14:-

This is what the Lord says: 'When seventy years are completed for Babylon, I will come to you and fulfil my gracious promise to bring you back to this place. For I know the plans I have for you,' declares the Lord, 'plans to prosper you and not to harm you, plans to give you hope and a future. Then you will call upon me and come and pray to me, and I will listen to you. You will seek me and find me when you seek me with all your heart. I will be found by you,' declares the Lord, 'and will bring you back from captivity. I will gather you from all the nations and places where I have banished you,' declares the Lord, 'and will bring you back to the place from which I carried you into exile.'

Israel's anticipated response is stated even more clearly in connection with the fall of Babylon in Jeremiah 50:4,5 and 20:-

'In those days, at that time,' declares the Lord, 'the people of Israel and the people of Judah together will go in tears to seek the Lord their God. They will ask the way to Zion and turn their faces towards it. They will come and bind themselves to the Lord in an everlasting covenant that will not be forgotten' ... 'In those days, at that time,' declares the Lord, 'search will be made for Israel's guilt, but there will be none, and for the sins of Judah, but none will be found, for I will forgive the remnant I spare.'

Israel responds with true repentance as in Hosea,

and their restoration and forgiveness are full and final as in Isaiah. The restoration of both houses of Israel is described in glowing terms in Jeremiah 30-31 with more of the same in chapters 32-33. The new (everlasting) covenant with the house of Israel and the house of Judah is also described. Another example of Ephraim's repentant prayer while in captivity is to be found in Jeremiah 31:18-19:

> 'You disciplined me like an unruly calf, and I have been disciplined. Restore me, and I will return, because you are the Lord my God. After I strayed, I repented; after I came to understand, I beat my breast. I was ashamed and humiliated because I bore the disgrace of my youth'

And the Lord's gracious response in the next verse:-

> 'Is not Ephraim my dear son, the child in whom I delight? Though I often speak against him, I still remember him. Therefore my heart yearns for him; I have

great compassion for him,' declares the Lord.

And the wonderful result in verses 8-9:-

> See, I will bring them from the land of the north and gather them from the ends of the earth. Among them will be the blind and the lame, expectant mothers and women in labour; a great throng will return. They will come with weeping; they will pray as I bring them back. I will lead them beside streams of water on a level path where they will not stumble, because I am Israel's father, and Ephraim is my firstborn son.

Admittedly there is a certain timelessness about all this. For Jeremiah it took the form of a pleasant dream from which he periodically awoke (Jeremiah 31:26). But the fall and desolation of Babylon are firmly placed by Jeremiah at the end of the seventy years (Jeremiah 25:12), and the restoration of Israel was expected to synchronise with that event (Jeremiah 29:10; 50:4-5,20). This is when Israel might have been restored to favour, their sins forgiven and forgotten, and their hearts and minds renewed in accordance with the new covenant which the Lord will make with the house of Israel and with the house of Judah (Jeremiah 31:31-34).

The seventy years of Babylonian domination began in the first year of Nebuchadnezzar, 605 BC. They should therefore have ended in 536 on inclusive reckoning or 535. But, so far as one can tell, nothing at all happened in 536 or 535. Babylon had already fallen on 12 October 539, three years too soon, and Cyrus' decree permitting the Jews to return was issued in the first year of his reign, in 538 or 536. The return itself was a very modest affair, the total number being only 42,360, besides 7,337 male and female slaves (Ezra 2:64).

The fall of Babylon bore no resemblance to the violent and cataclysmic downfall described in Jeremiah 50-51. According to the Cyrus Cylinder,

"Without battle and conflict he (Marduk) permitted him (Cyrus) to enter Babylon. He spared his city Babylon a calamity."

As described by Jeremiah it was nothing if not calamitous.

The Lord seems to be saying,

> "You have missed your opportunity. My promises cannot be fulfilled at this time because you have not turned to me with all your heart and repented of your wickedness. Everything I have said will be fulfilled in due course, but because of your continued disobedience it will not be for a long time."

In the short term Jeremiah's prophecies were fulfilled no more than Isaiah's. The seventy years, the fall of Babylon and the restoration of Israel are three important areas where the historical 'fulfilments' fell far short of what one would expect from reading Jeremiah. Another case of incomplete fulfilment is the prediction in

Jeremiah 27:7 that all nations would serve Nebuchadnezzar, his son and his son's son "until the time for his land comes". In point of history no son's son of Nebuchadnezzar ever sat on the throne of Babylon, and even his son, Amel-Marduk, did so for only two years (561-560 BC). The non-fulfilment of these prophecies simply reflects Israel's failure to repent and turn to the Lord.

Ezekiel

Ezekiel

A consistent expectation has been found in Isaiah and Jeremiah that Israel's restoration to fame and fortune would, hopefully, take place at the end of the Babylonian exile. Isaiah even placed the sacrificial death of the Servant in the course of the Exile, since there could be no restoration for Israel before their sins had been atoned for. All this however came to nothing because Israel failed to learn the lesson which their troubles were designed to teach them, failed to repent of their sin and turn to the Lord for forgiveness.

The same expectation is to be found in all the pre-exilic prophets, as well as in Ezekiel who prophesied during the Exile itself. Ezekiel 11:16-21; 36:22-38, and 37:1-28 are three passages which speak of Israel's restoration and transformation on their return to Palestine after the Exile. One passage will suffice, Ezekiel 37:21-23:-

This is what the Sovereign Lord says: I

will take the Israelites out of the nations where they have gone. I will gather them from all around and bring them back into their own land. I will make them one nation in the land, on the mountains of Israel. There will be one king over all of them and they will never again be two nations or be divided into two kingdoms. They will no longer defile themselves with their idols and vile images or with any of their offences, for I will save them from their sinful backsliding, and I will cleanse them. They will be my people, and I will be their God.

Daniel

Daniel

It was in the first year of Darius the Mede (538 BC) that Daniel set his face to the Lord, and pleaded with Him with fasting, sackcloth and ashes. Already Babylon had fallen to the Medes and Persians in the previous year, but the seventy years revealed to Jeremiah had not yet run out (Daniel 9:1-3). Could it be that Israel's promised destiny was about to materialize?

Daniel's prayer is one of contrite confession and repentance on behalf of himself and the nation. He acknowledges the justness of all that had happened to Jerusalem and themselves. He admits the persistent rebellion and disobedience of which they were guilty. He cries to the Lord for forgiveness and to have regard for the desolation of the city which bears His name. He asks the Lord to look with favour on His desolate sanctuary. He prays,

"O Lord, listen! O Lord, forgive! O Lord, hear and act! For your sake, O my God, do not delay, because your city and your people bear your name."

While he was still praying the angel Gabriel was sent with the answer he craved. In essence Gabriel's answer was

"No, not now, but Yes, in 490 years time".

The Lord's six-fold blessing on the people and the holy city would not now be experienced until after the decreed duration of "Seventy sevens". See Daniel 9:25-27.

From the issuing of the decree to restore and rebuild Jerusalem until the Anointed One, the ruler, comes, there will be seven 'sevens', and sixty-two 'sevens'. It will be rebuilt with streets and a trench, but in times of trouble. After the sixty-two 'sevens', the Anointed One will be cut off and will have nothing .... He (the coming prince) will confirm a covenant with many for one 'seven' ...

Without going into details of chronology, two things at least lie on the surface. The seventy sevens are divided 7, 62 and 1, and the Anointed One, their Messiah, will be cut off after the 62 sevens. We have therefore 7 sevens during which Jerusalem would be rebuilt with streets and moat, a further 62 sevens until the Anointed One is cut off, and a final one seven during which a coming ruler will perpetrate all sorts of enormities.[3]

The nature of the sevens, the time measure intended, is not recorded in so many words, but it does not seem possible to understand them in other way than years. This still leaves undecided whether they are solar years, lunar years, or luni-solar years of 360 days. In any event the Crucifixion is placed 69 sevens of years (483 years) after the decree to restore and rebuild Jerusalem, and with the complete Messianic rest placed only seven years after that. In other

---

[3] For more on this see *Daniel's Seventy Sevens: A Recalculation* by Michael Penny, published by The Open Bible Trust.

words, according to the revised prophetic programme revealed to Daniel, the Kingdom age should have already begun in AD 39-40, only seven years after the Crucifixion.

Does not this throw a flood of light on John the Baptist's sensational announcement repeated soon after by Jesus Himself (Matthew 4:17) and by His disciples (Matthew 10:7)? When this announcement was first made (in AD 28/29) there were only some four years to run before the 'cutting off' of the Messiah, and only eleven years before the setting up of the Kingdom which would never be destroyed (Daniel 2:44). No wonder they spoke with the urgency they did.

The
Gospels

The Gospels

The same urgency and immediacy is expressed by our Lord in Matthew 10:23,

> "I tell you the truth, you will not finish going through the cities of Israel before the Son of Man comes."

At this stage, so close was the coming of the Son of man, that a ministry to the nations was not even contemplated. The disciples are expressly told,

> "Do not go among the Gentiles (nations) or enter any town of the Samaritans. Go rather to the lost sheep of Israel" (Matthew 10:5-6).

When, however, verses 17-22 of this chapter are repeated in the Mount of Olives discourse (Mark 13:9-13) it is explicitly added,

> "And the gospel must first be preached to

all nations" (Mark 13:10).

At the very least, this expresses a change of policy, a change of direction, from what was contemplated in Matthew 10. Then it was Israel only (not even the Samaritans, let alone the nations), now *all* nations! Then it was only a very short time before the coming of the Son of Man (10:23), now a generation (but no more, Mark 13:30) before they would see the Son of Man coming in the clouds with great power and glory.

The same interval of one generation is expressed in Matthew 16:28,

> "I tell you the truth, some who are standing here will not taste death before they see the Son of Man coming in his kingdom."

In these statements we discern a shift from very soon (Matthew 10) to about a generation, from the short time presupposed by Daniel 9:24 to a rather longer period.

Already, it would seem, only two years into our

Lord's ministry, the last seven of years had been severed from the preceding sixty-nine. But at this stage it was only postponed for one generation during which the Jews were given an extended period in which to repent and to receive the Lord Jesus as their awaited Messiah.

All through the book of Acts this opportunity was still open to them. It was not until Acts 28 that this avenue was finally closed. Instead of the Son of Man coming in power and glory as anticipated in Matthew 10 and Mark 13, what in fact did they experience? The whole terrible sequence of events had been clearly foreseen by our Lord:-

> As he approached Jerusalem and saw the city, he wept over it and said, 'If you, even you, had only known on this day what would bring you peace - but now it is hidden from your eyes. The days will come upon you when your enemies will build an embankment against you and encircle you and hem you in on every side. They will dash you to the ground, you and the

children within your walls. They will not leave one stone on another, because you did not recognise the time of God's coming to you.' (Luke 19:41-44)

As on previous occasions, from the days of Joshua onwards, they did not recognise the time of God's coming, the time of their visitation. But this time the offer of Sabbath-rest was not simply postponed for a brief period, it was put on hold for about two thousand years. The Jewish people went out into the cold, *lo-ammi* and *lo-ruhamah*, not God's people and not pitied, and in their place a new company of believers began to be called out, a body which recognises no distinction between Jew and Gentile and whose blessing is in the heavenly places rather than the earthly or heavenly Jerusalem. Not until the Church Age comes to an end will the Jews get another opportunity to enter their own time of rest.

Evangelical opinion

Evangelical opinion

Evangelical commentators do not know what to do with Matthew 10:23; 16:28 and 24:34. Michael Green for example, in *The Bible Speaks Today* series, conveniently passes over Matthew 10:23 without comment. For Matthew 16:28 he offers a number of possible interpretations, his preference being for

> "the cross and resurrection, which will demonstrate that the King has entered on his kingly rule."

At Matthew 24:34 he launches into a scathing repudiation of date-setting, under cover of which he ducks out of saying anything positive himself. He is very positive however that

> "Jesus gave no political predictions whatsoever for Israel,"

that

"Always in the New Testament the church takes over the role of Israel in the Old,"

and that

"the physical return of Israel ... is theologically irrelevant."

But is it not far better to take these references at their face value? The Son of Man might well have returned in power and great glory before the disciples had finished evangelising the towns and hamlets of Israel. In fact, if Daniel's time schedule had been adhered to, this is precisely what would have happened. He might also have returned on the clouds before the demise of the generation then living if the Jews had repented and accepted the Lord Jesus as their Messiah before the end of the period covered by Acts.

It should however be noted that these verses do not say with absolute definiteness that the Lord will return within the time-limit stated. The Greek construction is deliberately indefinite. On Matthew 16:28

The Companion Bible comments, "The particle *an,* with the Subjunctive Mood, gives this a hypothetical force,"

and on Matthew 24:34,

"Here the Gr. *an,* and the Subj. Mood, marking the uncertainty, which was conditional on the repentance of the nation."

And the same applies to Matthew 10:23 even though the particle *an*[4] is omitted there. Bullinger gives a more extended treatment of these verses in his book *The Foundations of Dispensational Truth,*[5] pages 60-66.

At each stage in Israel's history, when their

---

[4] For a more detailed treatment of this subject see pages 79-85 of *40 Problem Passages* by Michael Penny, published by The Open Bible Trust
[5] Published by The Open Bible Trust and available as a hard-back and an eBook.

promised rest was offered them, they refused to accept it for reasons of unbelief and misunderstanding. What took place in the New Testament was the same in principle as had happened repeatedly in the Old. However their rejection now was all the more heinous in that God's Son and Heir was present in their midst and He was the One they rejected. When they killed the Son and Heir God's vineyard was put into the hands of other tenants (Matthew 21:33-41). Israel's promised future must now await the expiry of this tenancy.

The *a*-millennial obsession has dominated theological opinion since the earliest times and is still entrenched in evangelical thinking. The dispensational alternative has made little impact on our theological colleges and faculties, in this country at least. It does not seem to worry them that so much of the Old Testament, including vast tracts of the prophetic scriptures, is rendered null and void if their position is correct.

The glorious vision of Jerusalem raised up and enlarged, with the wealth and worship of the nations pouring into it (Isaiah 2:2-4; 49:19-21; 54:1-3; 60:3-14; Zechariah 14:10,16), the arid Arabah awash with water flowing from the Temple precincts, the Dead Sea itself swarming with living creatures and teeming with fish (Ezekiel 47) - why is all this on record if the land and people of Israel will never be restored?

This restoration will not be in some ethereal New Jerusalem, but in the geographically plotted stretch of land promised to Abraham and his descendants. And what about the Temple itself? Why was Ezekiel inspired to devote eight chapters detailing its dimensions and appointments if no such temple would ever be built? Why did he describe the boundaries of the Promised Land and the portions which would be allotted to each tribe if the physical return of Israel is theologically irrelevant?

The final offer

The final offer

That Israel will have one more opportunity and this opportunity they will embrace, is taught (or presupposed) in every book of the Bible. From Moses to Malachi and from Matthew to Revelation Israel's repentance and restoration is a recurring theme. It is assured by the faithfulness and constancy of God Himself, for His honour and reputation are at stake.

> "For my own sake, for my own sake, I do this,"

the Lord says.

> "How can I let myself be defamed? I will not yield my glory to another." (Isaiah 48:11)

Ezekiel makes the point that God's main concern is His holy name. Wherever the people of Israel went among the nations they profaned His holy name, for it was said of them,

> "These are the Lord's people, and yet they had to leave his land" (Ezekiel 36:20).

Hence,

> "This is what the Sovereign Lord says: It is not for your sake, O house of Israel, that I am going to do these things, but for the sake of my holy name, which you have profaned among the nations where you have gone. I will show the holiness of my great name ..." (Ezekiel 36:22-23).

And again in verse 32;

> "I want you to know that I am not doing this for your sake, declares the Sovereign Lord."

Israel's repentance will not come out of the blue by Divine fiat. It will be wrenched from them in the cauldron of overwhelming adversity and the threat of national extinction. Zechariah 13:8-9 says,

> "In the whole land," declares the Lord, "two-thirds will be struck down and perish; yet one-third will be left in it. This third I will bring into the fire; I will refine them like silver and test them like gold. They will call on my name and I will answer them."

Likewise Hosea 5:15,

> "I will go back to my place until they admit their guilt. And they will seek my face; in their misery they will earnestly seek me."

And Jeremiah 30:7;

"How awful that day will be! None will be like it. It will be a time of trouble for Jacob, but he will be saved out of it."

Israel's restoration is as predictable as the fixed orbits of the sun, moon and stars, as certain as man's abiding ignorance of outer space and the earth's core, and as irrevocable as the elusive laws which determine the motion of the sea and its waves.

> "Only if these decrees vanish from my sight," declares the Lord, "will the descendants of Israel ever cease to be a nation before me ... Only if the heavens above can be measured and the foundations of the earth below be searched out will I reject all the descendants of Israel because of all they have done," declares the Lord (Jeremiah 31:35-37).

It is not simply the conversion of "all Israel" and their joining the Christian church which the prophet has in mind, but their continuation against all the odds as a distinct and separate nation. Jerusalem also, within defined and measurable boundaries ...

> "will never again be uprooted or demolished" (Jeremiah 31:31:38-40).

Yes, Israel will be humbled and restored. No,

their Sabbath-rest will not be permanently postponed. Next time round Jacob will prevail, and so will the Lord who will then have His way with His chosen people.

Conclusion

Conclusion

The impression may have been conveyed that God is constantly changing His mind, that He is lacking in purpose and resolve, or that He is too easily swayed by human unbelief and failure. But that would be a completely wrong impression.

A God who knows the end from the beginning cannot be taken by surprise. He knew exactly how Adam would react before He ever created him, exactly how Israel would rebel before He made the choice of their forefathers, exactly how each one of us would behave before we were born. The wonder is that He went ahead with His plan in spite of having this knowledge. Martyn Lloyd Jones has written:

> It is surely the most consoling fact one can ever discover at a time such as this, that God's plan was made perfect and complete before the world was made, before the time process began. It is there irrespective of all that is happening; and it is certain. There is

nothing contingent about God's plan. God never had to improvise, or modify His policy because of what someone else has done. It was a plan before the beginning of the ages, before time itself was created. It is an eternal purpose.

God's invitations are no less genuine because He knows they will be declined; Israel's guilt no less culpable because it fulfils

"God's set purpose and foreknowledge" (Acts 2:23).

If Joshua had given them rest, God would not have spoken later about another day. But there was no way Joshua could have given them rest, or David, or even Christ at His first coming. God's over-arching, all-embracing plan digests every failure of man and drives it on to its predetermined conclusion.

More on Israel

More on Israel

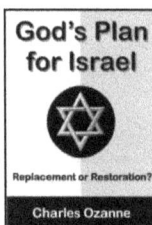

God's Plan for Israel: Replacement or Restoration?
By Charles Ozanne

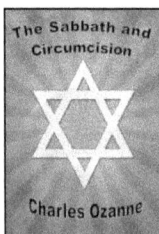

The Sabbath and Circumcision
By Charles Ozanne

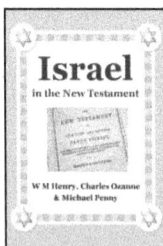

Israel in the New Testament
With contributions from Charles Ozanne, W.M. Henry and Michael Penny

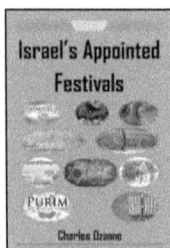

Israel's Appointed Festivals
By Charles Ozanne

Further details of all the books mentioned on these pages can be seen on

www.obt.org.uk

These can be ordered from that website and also from

The Open Bible Trust,
Fordland Mount,
Upper Basildon, Reading,
RG8 8LU, UK.

They are also available as eBooks from Amazon Kindle and the Apple iBookstore, and also as KDP paperbacks from Amazon.

About the
Author

About the Author

Charles Ozanne was born in Crowborough, Sussex, in 1936. He read Theology at Oxford before undertaking research in the book of Revelation for his PhD at the University of Manchester under F. F. Bruce.

Some of his recent publications for the Open Bible Trust have been a commentary on Daniel, entitled *Empires of the End-Time;* a critique of Replacement Theology entitled *God's Plan for Israel: Replacement or Restoration?* And a work looking at *The Sabbath and Circumcision.* A major work, *The Believer's Guide to Bible Chronology* has been published by *Authorhouse.* *H*owever, it is available from the Open Bible Trust.

His latest work is *Understanding the New Testament.* A well-written and well-presented commentary on the whole of the New Testament, showing that each of the 27 documents, although distinctive, fit into an overall pattern. For further details of this latest book see next page.

Understanding
The New Testament

son God
came I David make
Israel Lord one man
house like sons man
shall land people

From Matthew
to Revelation

Charles Ozanne

Understanding
The New Testament
From Matthew to Revelation

The New Testament is a single book made up of twenty-seven interrelated parts. Having a good overview of the whole increases our appreciation of the parts, but, on the other hand, having a more detailed knowledge of the parts gives us a better understanding of the whole!

Charles Ozanne does a good job in giving the reader a guided tour through the New Testament. He briefly explains the purpose of each book and gives a synopsis of its teaching yet, all the while, keeping an eye on how it fits into the overall picture.

Charles Ozanne is a regular contributor to
Search magazine

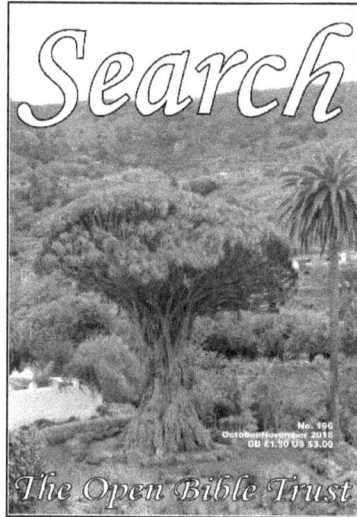

Also by Charles Ozanne

The following is a selection.

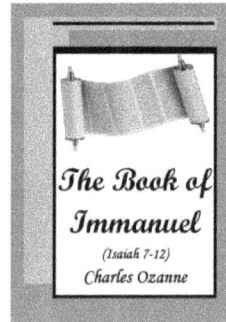

Sensational Truth in Ephesians

Amos: The Lion has roared

The Book of Immaneul
(Isaiah 7-12)

****

Further details of all the books mentioned on these pages can be seen on

www.obt.org.uk

These can be ordered from that website and also from

The Open Bible Trust,
Fordland Mount,
Upper Basildon, Reading,
RG8 8LU, UK.

They are also available as eBooks from Amazon Kindle and the Apple iBookstore, and also as KDP paperbacks from Amazon.

More by Charles Ozanne

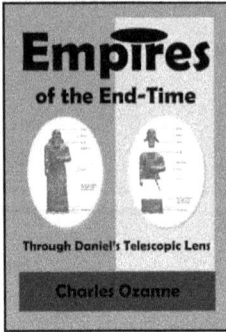

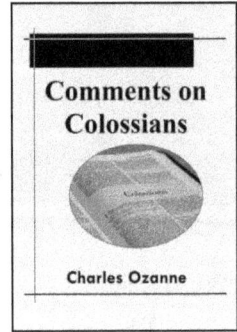

Empires
of the End-Time

Through Daniel's Telescopic Lens

Charles Ozanne

Baptism
- rite & reality -

Charles Ozanne

**Comments on
Colossians**

Charles Ozanne

Empires of the End-Times
Through Daniel's Telescopic Lens

Baptism:
Rite and reality

Comments on Colossians

****

**These books are also available as
eBooks from Amazon and Apple**

And as KDP paperback from Amazon

About this book

Israel's Missed Opportunities
... and lost privileges

Israel had been promised by God a 'time of rest'. Charles Ozanne demonstrates that this was offered to them time and again in the course of their long history, only to be forfeited on each occasion.

The most disastrous of Israel's *missed opportunities* was their failure to recognise their Messiah. They rejected Him when He graced them with His presence, and they rejected Him in the years following when the truth of Him being their Messiah was persuasively proclaimed to them by His faithful disciples. The abiding consequences for them of that missed opportunity are still with us today.

However, God has not given up on His erstwhile people. Sometime in the future they will be given a final opportunity to receive the Lord Jesus as their Messiah, and this time they will unreservedly accept Him ... and with what marvellous results!

Publications of The Open Bible Trust must be in accordance with its evangelical, fundamental and dispensational basis. However, beyond this minimum, writers are free to express whatever beliefs they may have as their own understanding, provided that the aim in so doing is to further the object of The Open Bible Trust. A copy of the doctrinal basis is available on **www.obt.org.uk** or from:

THE OPEN BIBLE TRUST
Fordland Mount, Upper Basildon,
Reading, RG8 8LU, UK

www.ingramcontent.com/pod-product-compliance
Lightning Source LLC
Chambersburg PA
CBHW070538030426
42337CB00016B/2258